CONTENTS

Materials

There are many different techniques and methods for using tissue paper in works of art. The aim of this book is to give even more ideas for creating a variety of surfaces using different tissue papers combined with acrylic mediums, foils and a mixture of colouring agents.

A majority of these surfaces can be used as stand-alone pieces but they will all be enhanced with further embellishment in the way of stitch, beads or additional mixed media products and techniques.

Although you will find here basic instructions for creating a number of finished pieces, the intention of this book is to show you the techniques used to achieve these surfaces. They can then be used for your own projects or incorporated into larger pieces of work.

Use this book as a starting point. Challenge yourself to take them further. Don't stop with what you see on these pages. Rather, add further ideas of your own using products and materials that you have in your stash.

Most of all, give yourself permission to take time to experiment, to play and to have fun!

Many of the techniques described in this book can be achieved using recycled tissue (that crumpled piece that your new shoes were wrapped up in) and fusible webbing. However, there are almost as many different varieties of tissue paper as there are backgrounds and it's worth trying some of the ones described below.

< *Book cover created using techniques from Section 3: Magnificent Metallic Surfaces.*

Tissue papers

The good thing is that none of these will break the bank. Here are some to try:

- Abaca tissue
- Teabag tissue
- Speciality tissues
- Gift wrap tissue (plain, patterned, coloured, metallic)
- Dressmaking pattern tissue

Abaca tissue, also known as Tissuetex, repair tissue and wet strength tissue, is a wonderful all-rounder. It can be painted, sponged, printed, stitched, ripped, layered, glued and even used for batik. After it has been coloured and dried, if you scrunch it up and smooth it out again, the fibres will soften. It comes in two different weights: 9gm and 22gm.

Teabag tissue will bond to itself if ironed in layers. Remember this if you ever try to cut corners by ironing the creases out of a stash of teabag tissue with several layers at a time!

Speciality tissues include Mulberry, Japanese, Lokta and many more. They range from delicate and translucent to heavily textured. Some may have fibres, skeleton leaves or threads embedded into the surface. They can be quite expensive but are certain to give any piece of work the 'wow' factor.

Gift wrap tissue is at the other end of the scale and the plain white can usually be obtained for nothing. Also available in bright colours, patterned or with a metallic finish, it bonds well and crumples easily but will tear if not treated carefully when using wet mediums.

Dressmaking pattern tissue, especially the brown variety, is an excellent tissue to use. It is quite readily available as we all seem to have old patterns stashed away somewhere, and it's a great way of recycling. This tissue will withstand a lot more liquid than the inexpensive gift wrap tissue but still needs to be treated with care. The pre-printed lines on the patterns can be used successfully as a design feature if desired and with the brown tissue paper you have the advantage of a semi-aged surface to work on before you begin.

Try and experiment with as many of these as you can until you find the one that is right for you and the project you are working on.

> Dressmaking pattern tissue is readily available and is a great way of recycling.

CUT
COUPEZ
CORTE

Bonding agents

Several bonding agents are available to use when bonding tissue paper to a surface, some of which can give a very different effect even when using the same technique.

- Bondaweb/Wonder Under
- Fuse FX/Gossamer Fuse/Misty Fuse
- Bonding Powder
- 606 Spray
- PVA glue/acrylic gels and mediums

Bondaweb/Wonder Under fusible webbing is generally the one used throughout the samples in this book. It is very easy to use and works really well for the techniques shown. It can be coloured before application.

Fuse FX, Gossamer Fuse and Misty Fuse, available in black and white, will also work exceptionally well, especially with a foil base, giving a lacy effect rather than a solid block (which can happen with other adhesives). The white can be coloured in the same way as the Bondaweb/Wonder Under. Lay it on baking parchment prior to colouring and leave until thoroughly dry before removing it.

Bonding Powder and 606 Spray are useful as they can be applied only to the areas that you wish the tissue paper to adhere to. They are also extremely useful when you wish to apply foil only in a certain area or on a small part of a design.

PVA glue/acrylic gels and mediums also have their place in bonding tissue to fabric. In some cases they will make the resulting fabric slightly stiffer than fusible webbing would and, of course, you will need to wait until the adhesive is dry before being able to work on the surface.

With maybe a few exceptions, the choice of bonding agent will depend on the technique used but, again, try and experiment with as many as you can, making a note of the different effects for future use.

Colouring agents

Virtually any colouring mediums can be used, depending on the intended use of your created piece of work. You will need to consider the following points:

- Generally speaking, the samples and techniques throughout this book use fluid acrylic paints, silk paints, Brusho powders and inks and Procion dyes.
- All the mediums will have been watered down to a certain extent.
- Use the Procion dye as a watercolour paint. There's no need to add fixatives, but keep in mind that even unfixed dye will stain your hands and clothes.
- Try to be economical when applying your colour. If it is too light, you can always add a second coat but it is virtually impossible to remove too much colour.

SECTION 1:
Basic Techniques

Bonding to fabric

The simplest way of creating a new surface using tissue paper is to bond it to a base fabric. Any of the bonding agents mentioned previously can be used, depending on the effect you are trying to achieve. Almost any type of fabric will work, from a lightweight cotton muslin to a heavyweight pelmet Vilene. The created fabric can then be coloured using a variety of mediums to achieve the finish you require.

Why not create a postcard-size folded pocket book using a fusible webbing to bond gift wrap tissue paper to Lutradur 30 weight? A lightweight Vilene interfacing or a similar weight openweave fabric could be used in place of the Lutradur.

∧ *Folded pocket book coloured with fluid acrylic paints.*

To make the book, two pieces of tissue paper fabric have been coloured and bonded together before applying a finishing coat.

Here's how:

1. Place the fusible webbing on top of the piece of Lutradur or similar. Make sure that the webbing is paper side up.

2. Set the iron midway between the wool and cotton setting and start at the centre of the webbing, working your way out towards the edges, pressing lightly as you go. This will help to prevent the Lutradur from creasing underneath. If the Lutradur does crease, do not be tempted to flip the fabric over and press from the other side. As the Lutradur is very fine, some of the webbing adhesive goes right through the surface and the iron will stick to it.

< *Procion dye was used to colour the gift wrap tissue for this book. A light coat of acrylic varnish was applied to make the surface shine.*

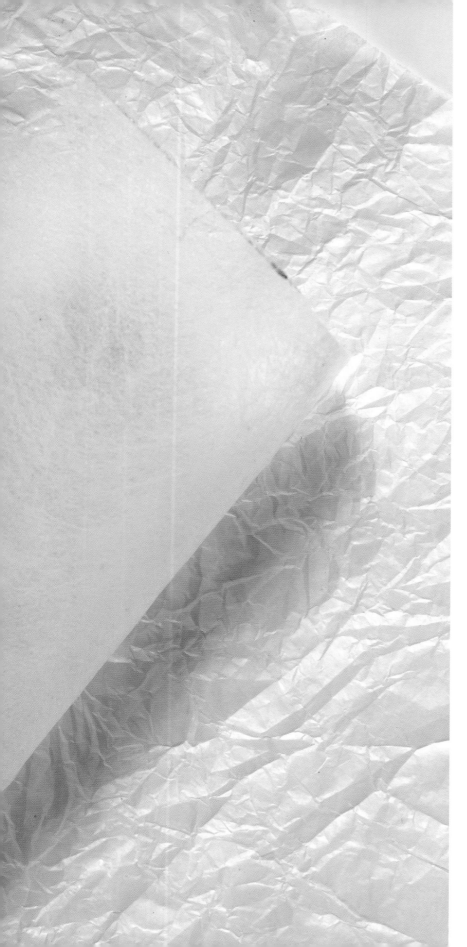

3. Carefully peel the backing paper away. Leaving the fusible webbing to cool down makes it easier to remove the backing paper.

4. Take a sheet of tissue paper, crumple it and, very carefully, unfold it again. Crumpling the tissue gives the surface added interest.

5. Place the tissue on top of the bonded Lutradur and iron once again, starting at the centre of the tissue paper and working towards the edges.

6. Use a patting motion with the iron until you have covered the whole surface as this will help prevent creasing. Then iron gently all over to eliminate any air pockets.

7. Turn the fabric over and cut away the excess tissue paper, close to the edges of the Lutradur.

Colouring

This surface can be coloured with almost any colouring medium you wish. If using Procion dyes, silk dyes, Brusho powders etc. try not to make the surface too wet or it may affect the fusible webbing that has come through the back of the Lutradur. There is also a possibility that the tissue paper will tear.

The tissue may bubble up in places when applying the wet medium. It will go back down again once the fabric is dry and a light press with the iron will ensure it is attached once more to the backing fabric.

< *Place the crumpled gift wrap on top of the bonded Lutradur and press gently with a warm iron.*

The colouring mediums just mentioned have a tendency to go dull once they dry but this can be rectified by adding a layer of acrylic varnish, either gloss or matt, or acrylic wax. Other mediums could also be used as a top layer, such as PVA, Gel Medium, Mod Podge etc. Some colouring mediums, such as acrylic paint, may not need a top layer to make the colours glow.

Making the book

One piece of fabric 36 x 43 cm (14 x 17 in) makes a pocket book for holding postcards. It is best to make the fabric a little larger and then cut it to size. Cut two sheets of fabric and, when thoroughly dry, fuse them together before adding the top layer of varnish, wax or other medium. You should find there is still enough fusible webbing on the back of the Lutradur to enable the two pieces to adhere together. Work like this:

1. Place baking parchment on your ironing surface and lay one piece of fabric face down on the parchment. Place the second piece of fabric on top, right side facing up, lining up the edges of the Lutradur as closely as possible. Lay another piece of baking parchment on the fabric surface and iron to fuse the two sheets together. As before, pat the iron down onto the surface, starting at the centre and working outwards before ironing over the piece of fabric in the usual way. Pay particular attention to the edges.

2. Make sure the iron does not come into contact with the coloured surface, especially if you have used acrylic paints, or it may be ruined.

3. The fabric can now be cut to the size required.

Although this is an optional stage, it is a good idea to machine stitch around the edges of the fabric before folding into shape, as lots of handling can sometimes make the two sheets of fabric pull apart.

The following samples were coloured with Procion dye and looked quite dull to begin with. However, after fusing the two sheets together, a layer of acrylic gloss varnish was added and the colour intensified immediately.

∧ *Machine stitching the edges helps to prevent the fabric pulling apart.*

∧ *Before varnish.*

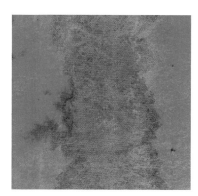

∧ *After varnish.*

If using an acrylic varnish or any other acrylic medium to seal the surface, leave the finished fabric to air-dry for a few days before folding or it may stick to itself.

Once the fabric is folded to make the pocket book and embellished further, it looks totally different again.

These pocket books can be embellished in many ways. You will find some ideas for this later in the book. The one shown left, has added text.

∧ *Folded pocket books made with fabric created from gift wrap tissue paper bonded onto Lutradur 30 weight, painted with a variety of mediums and finishes.*

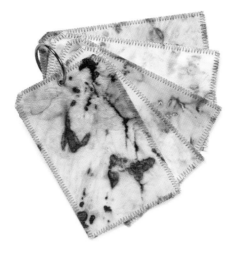

Rusted tissue paper

Rusted tissue paper is yet another option for colouring the surface. A heavyweight tissue paper such as Abaca would be the best choice. You could always try bonding two lighter-weight sheets of tissue together but there is still a possibility that it will disintegrate, as you need to keep the tissue wet throughout the rusting process.

For a very simple method of rusting, make a tightly wrapped parcel with the tissue paper using rusty wire or similar. Soak the tissue thoroughly and leave out in the sunshine for a few days. Water the parcel regularly to keep it moist at all times. After a few days, remove the wire carefully, unfold the tissue paper and leave to dry.

Once dry, any creases can be ironed out before use. The background of the tissue paper will turn a warm brown with some really interesting darker brown marks.

∧ Sheets of rusted Abaca tissue were tightly rolled and cut at an angle before attaching around a tube.

> TOP and BELOW:
> Journal and bag tags
> created from tissue
> paper bonded to a foiled
> surface and then painted.
> Embossing powder adds
> highlights.

Bonding to a foiled sur

The background surface, plain or coloure
can be foiled before bonding the tissue p
and adding further layers of colour. The f
background will then give a warm glow t
colours painted on the surface.

Most colouring mediums will work on thi.
surface but choose one that dries semi-
transparent to allow the foil to shine through.
Fluid acrylic paints, Procion dye, walnut ink and
writing ink are all worth experimenting with.

If the resulting colour is not quite as vibrant
as you would like, apply a layer of acrylic
varnish, medium or PVA glue to the surface.
This will really bring out the shine of the
foiled background.

Why not try using one of the lacy-type fusible
webbings to bond the foil to a previously
coloured background before applying the tissue
paper and adding colour to the surface?

Seal the surface first with an acrylic medium
or PVA glue if you do not want your top
colours mixing with the background colours.
And don't forget to flip the piece over and
look at the back, as this too can yield some
very interesting results.

< Dressmaking tissue paper was
  bonded to a foiled surface and
  coloured with fluid acrylic paints.
  A coat of acrylic varnish brought out
  the shine of the foiled background.

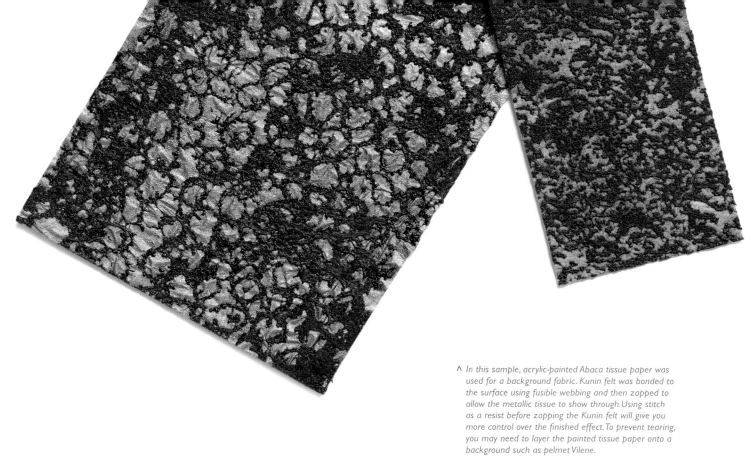

∧ In this sample, acrylic-painted Abaca tissue paper was used for a background fabric. Kunin felt was bonded to the surface using fusible webbing and then zapped to allow the metallic tissue to show through. Using stitch as a resist before zapping the Kunin felt will give you more control over the finished effect. To prevent tearing, you may need to layer the painted tissue paper onto a background such as pelmet Vilene.

Using painted tissue as a background

With care, most tissue papers can be painted before bonding to a fabric background. You will need to lay the paper on a plastic-covered surface before painting with your preferred medium. To make a more durable surface, two layers of the finer tissue papers could be bonded together before painting. Any paints used need to be of a fairly thin consistency. If they are too heavy, they tend to drag along the surface of the tissue, sometimes causing tears or holes to appear. Leave the painted sheet of tissue paper to dry thoroughly before carefully peeling from the plastic surface.

The resulting paper can now be bonded to a background fabric and stitched. If using acrylic paints, you will find the underneath surface – the one that is lying directly on top of the plastic sheet – will be very shiny. This is the surface that will be bonded to the background fabric if you are using the painted tissue as a surface on top of the background fabric.

Turning this around and using a 'zappable' acrylic felt, such as Kunin, gives interesting results if bonded **on top of** the painted side of the tissue. It can then be heated with a heat tool to show the treasure beneath.

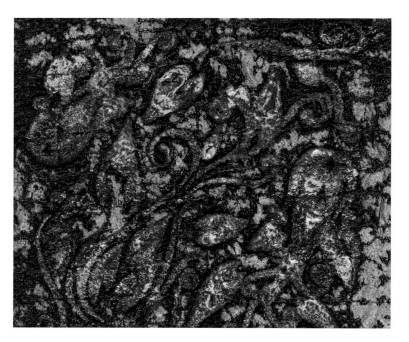

^ A light rub of Treasure Gold makes the stencilled design stand out from the background.

A polyester thread can been used so that the zapped surface is not too regimented. If a more defined stitch pattern is required, use a cotton thread that will not melt with the heat.

Try stencilling or screening a design on the Kunin felt surface before burning back, to act as a resist. The Abaca tissue in the photo was coloured with metallic paints before the Kunin felt was stitched onto the surface. Black gesso, pushed through a stencil and left to dry, acts as a resist when zapped with the heat tool. Any medium that is thick enough to stencil with can be used. Choose a reasonably bold design, as anything with too much detail will be lost. A light rub of Treasure Gold makes the stencilled design stand out from the background.

An interesting effect can be achieved using the same coloured acrylic paint for the stencilled design that you have used for colouring the tissue paper. Alternatively black acrylic paint could be used with heat transfer foil lightly ironed on the surface as above.

Take care when ironing the foil on an acrylic surface as occasionally the carrier paper will stick to the paint. The easiest way to foil an acrylic-painted surface without heat is to lay down the foil, coloured side up, and gently burnish it with a metal implement, such as the side of a spoon.

∧ Black acrylic paint was
stencilled onto the Kunin
felt before zapping. Heat
transfer foil, in three
different colours, was
ironed carefully onto the
surface.

> Detail of a vessel made from metallic-painted Abaca tissue
overlaid with Kunin felt. It was stitched and stencilled with
acrylic paint before zapping. Heat transfer foil was then
applied to the stencilled design.

You might like to try ironing the tissue pap[...] freezer paper before printing. Only iron ar[...] the edges; if you iron it completely, you wil[...] able to remove the tissue after printing.

To make a quiltie like the one shown bel[...] will need to construct a stitched backgro[...] ready to receive the print. In the photo, y[...] see that the central area was used to sh[...] the printed design. After the stitching, a layer of gesso was applied and when dry was coloured with acrylic paints.

Cotton duck is used here but any heavy cotton fabric is OK. Use up all those odd bits of patterned cotton fabric that you have in your stash, as the layers of paint will hide the patterning. Furnishing fabric is ideal as it is but, if you decide to use a thinner cotton, you will need to double it or bond two pieces together. What you are aiming for is a fabric that is thick enough to avoid the gesso and paints seeping through to the wadding.

Printed tissue paper

This technique works best with a photocopier or a laser printer. Alternatively, a waterproof pen or ballpoint allows you to trace your design or motif directly onto the tissue paper. Dressmaking pattern tissue is ideal and needs no special treatment. Pages from an inkjet printer need to be printed on 'best' setting and placed print side down on the surface (if using lettering, remember to reverse the image).

Whichever method you use, the tissue paper needs to be firmly affixed to a carrier sheet, as it is too thin to put through the copier or printer as it is. Iron the tissue paper first to remove any wrinkles. Either (a) use spraymount (but don't spray the whole sheet) or a glue stick along each edge, top and bottom, of a sheet of plain copy paper and attach the tissue paper, or (b) use masking tape to hold down each end. If the markings on dressmaking pattern tissue are an important part of your design, make sure the right side is facing up so that any pre-printed marks or text are facing the correct way.

> *The printed tissue used for this quiltie was first bonded to a background fabric. The areas to be 'coloured' with fabric were then outlined with machine stitching.*

Now to make the quiltie:

1. Decide how large your printed pattern area is going to be and leave a gap to that size. Mark your design onto the fabric using a pencil, as some inks tend to show through even after several layers of paint. The design itself can be as easy or as complicated as you wish.

2. Once your design is drawn, pin your fabric to a backing ready for machine stitching. A recycled blanket is excellent to use as a backing as the finished hanging is much firmer than it would be if you used wadding or batting. Use a light-coloured thread, either cotton or polyester and do not worry if your stitches are an uneven size as these will not be noticeable once the layers of gesso and paint are added.

3. Before adding gesso to your stitched quiltie, put masking tape all around the edges about 1 cm (¼ in) from the outside stitched line. You will need to paint right up to this line so that when you turn the edges over, there will be no white fabric showing through. Do not paint right up to the raw edges of the fabric as layers of gesso and paint will make it very difficult to sew through. Now paint with the gesso, using a light application in the central area, which will be stitched. Remove the masking tape as soon as you have finished. See above, right.

4. Now add a layer of white acrylic paint – just the ordinary variety, not fluid. This is really only necessary if you are using fluid acrylic paints to colour the surface. The layer of white acrylic allows you more time to work the coloured acrylics on the surface. Make sure the white paint is thoroughly dry before adding colour. When it is, paint the surface with acrylic paints in the colours of your choice. Make sure the area you have left for the tissue paper design is kept a very light colour or you may not be able to see the outline of the printed design.

5. Now stick the tissue paper design to the surface. Cut the design to fit the gap left in the stitching on the quiltie and use either polymer medium or PVA glue to attach the tissue paper to the background. Brush another layer of medium over the surface and rub this in with your fingertips to remove any air pockets. Don't rub too hard or the tissue may tear. Once the tissue paper is transparent and you can see the background colours, put to one side to dry totally. This may take a day or two depending on the weather.

6. Now choose your fabric to 'colour-in' parts of the central design. Most fabrics are suitable and metal shim is also an option. As this is a reverse appliqué process, the easiest way to make sure the coloured fabric is placed correctly is to outline the areas of the design that you are going to colour-in with machine stitching, using a black thread on the bobbin. Coloured fabric or metal is laid right side up over the design and held in place using masking tape. Working from the back and following the pre-stitched lines, this is then machined in place. Once completed, the excess fabric is cut as close as possible to the machine stitching. To prevent fraying, fusible webbing can be used on the fabric before stitching into place. Alternatively, a zigzag stitch can be used around the outside edges after the initial stitching and cutting. An alternative method to transfer a design to the tissue paper for this technique is to use a waterproof marker pen and trace your design or draw freehand onto the tissue. A waterproof marker pen is also ideal for adding any extra touches to your design after printing. Stamping your design with a waterproof ink would also work very well.

A design or text printed on tissue paper can be used in a number of ways.

The text for these vessels was printed on dressmaking pattern tissue paper and bonded to the surface using polymer medium after the vessels had been painted. A wash of fluid acrylic paint, which dries transparent, was applied to blend the text into the background.

Areas of this design, below, were 'coloured-in' with metallic paints and then highlighted with machine stitch.

The pieces described here use 'black only' printed designs, which work extremely well for this technique, but you could also have fun trying colour. Always make sure you use copyright-free images for your work.

∧ Vessels with insets using printed tissue paper which was bonded to the surface. These were painted with fluid acrylic paint, which had the effect of blending the text with the background.

> Text and images were used together in this detail of a larger piece of work.

SECTION 2:
Beyond the Basics

Foiled tissue paper

Printed tissue paper can also be foiled before using in a project. Again you will need a print from a laser printer or photocopier. The toner used in these machines is produced from a blend of plastic resins and will therefore melt once heat is applied, enabling the foil to have something to bond to. Use a fresh print for best results. Lay the foil over the printed surface, shiny side facing up, cover with baking parchment and iron on the hot setting. Remove the carrier paper and you will find that the foil has only adhered to the printed section. Keep the leftover foil and use as described below.

The inkjet version

If you don't have access to a laser printer, just take your inkjet print to the copy shop and have a black and white copy made. Foil this, as described above, and you will have a perfect negative image which will look great bonded to a dark background fabric. Printed tissue with the same design can be adhered to the foiled surface and finished with hand and machine stitching.

∧ A laser printer was used to print text onto Abaca tissue which was then foiled with heat transfer foil.

< Gold coloured heat transfer foil outlines these designs printed onto tissue paper which were then used to create book covers.

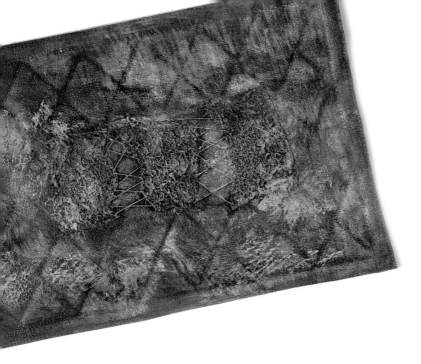

< Scrumpled tissue paper was machine stitched to this quiltie before layering with gesso and fluid acrylic paints. These small quilts are an ideal way to showcase a new technique and also allow you to practise your colouring techniques before embarking on a larger project.

Scrumpling

This technique was shown to me by Kim Thittichai. This is my version – perfect with tissue paper. The textured surfaces shown here were created by layering a piece of dissolvable Vilene with two pieces of fusible webbing.

1. Carefully remove the webbing from the backing sheet before placing on the Vilene. Lay the tissue paper on the top. The tissue papers shown in the materials section will work for this technique but the lighter-weight tissue papers will need to be bonded to fusible webbing before stitching or they may tear when stitched. Lightweight tissue papers will scrunch up more than the heavier-weight papers.

2. Using a polyester thread, machine stitch in tramlines (or a grid pattern) along the length of the layers. The closer the sewing lines are the more texture will be created.

3. With the tissue paper side facing up, use a steam iron on the hottest setting, hovering the iron above the fabric. Do not let the iron touch the fabric. The longer you steam the more the fabric will shrink.

The tissue paper can be painted either before or after the steaming process. Use water-based mediums to colour beforehand for the process to work correctly. If acrylic paint is applied too thickly, the steam will not penetrate the layers to enable the Vilene to shrink.

Depending on which colouring agent is being used, it may be a good idea to attach the fabric to a backing if painting after steaming: large quantities of wet mediums will dissolve the Vilene which can then become very sticky. Spraying the colour onto the steamed surface is also an option.

Foil can be bonded to the painted or unpainted tissue paper surface before machine stitching and steaming.

> This vessel was made from scrumpled tissue paper applied in patches to zapped Kunin felt. It was layered with gesso and white acrylic paint before being coloured with fluid acrylic paints.

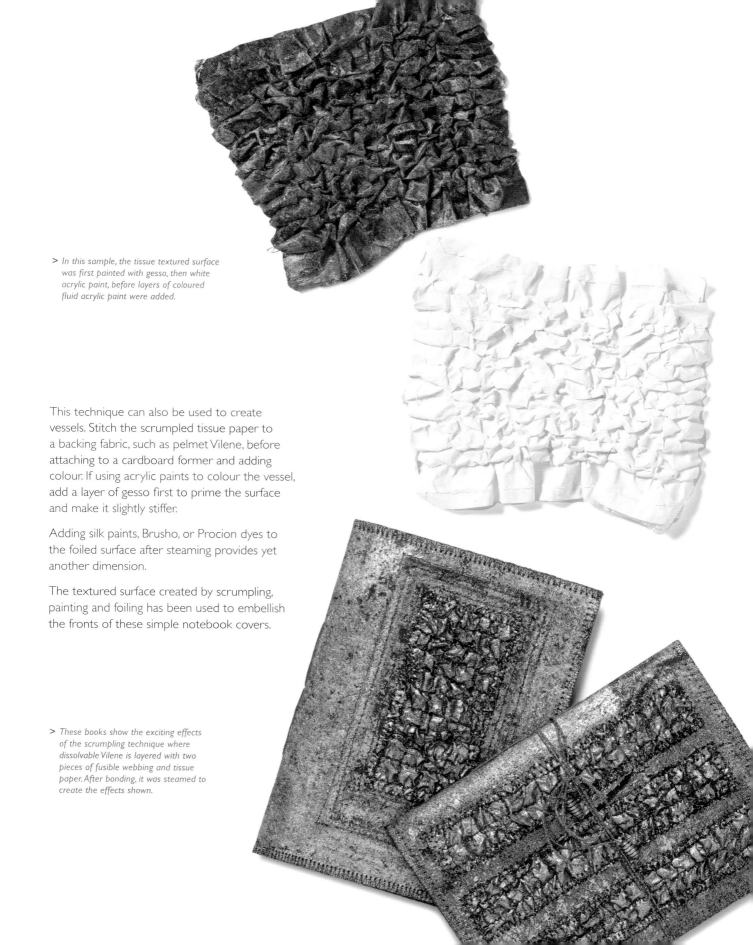

> In this sample, the tissue textured surface was first painted with gesso, then white acrylic paint, before layers of coloured fluid acrylic paint were added.

This technique can also be used to create vessels. Stitch the scrumpled tissue paper to a backing fabric, such as pelmet Vilene, before attaching to a cardboard former and adding colour. If using acrylic paints to colour the vessel, add a layer of gesso first to prime the surface and make it slightly stiffer.

Adding silk paints, Brusho, or Procion dyes to the foiled surface after steaming provides yet another dimension.

The textured surface created by scrumpling, painting and foiling has been used to embellish the fronts of these simple notebook covers.

> These books show the exciting effects of the scrumpling technique where dissolvable Vilene is layered with two pieces of fusible webbing and tissue paper. After bonding, it was steamed to create the effects shown.

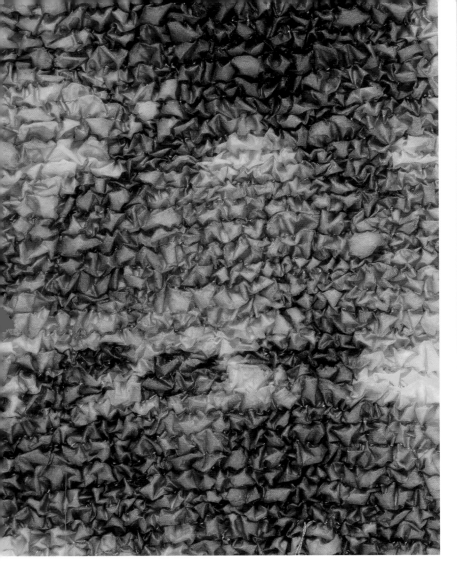

∧ *Silk painted polyester tissue.*

∧ *Heat distressable tissue coloured with disperse dyes before scrumpling.*

Heat distressable/ polyester tissue

This tissue paper is available in different weights from a very fine fabric-like tissue to a heavier weight which has the appearance of paper. It will react to heat in a similar way to Tyvek but is still pliable enough to be stitched into, by hand or machine, even after heating and shrinking.

Using this tissue paper can result in a really good effect for the scrumpling technique but, ideally, the colour needs to be applied before steaming as this tissue paper is basically water repellent and tends to resist most dyes and paints.

∧ *Silk painted polyester tissue.*

A reasonable effect can be achieved with silk paints, although you will find the underneath of the paper remains sticky. However, for other water-based colouring agents, you would need to coat the paper first with inkAID, or a similar product, which will inhibit the steaming process.

By far the best option for colour is to use transfer paints or disperse dyes to colour the surface before steaming. Paint the dyes onto copy paper and, once dry, lay face down onto the tissue. Cover with baking parchment and press with an iron on the wool setting. Do not let the iron touch the tissue paper or it will start to crinkle. Due to the low heat of the iron, it will take a while to activate the dyes but, once this starts to happen, the dye will transfer quite quickly to the tissue surface.

Keep ironing until the colour is the required depth. If using the lightweight tissue, place another piece underneath the surface that is being coloured. Some of the dye goes straight through the tissue and this way you will get a lighter print on the bottom piece.

Once the tissue has been transfer dyed, other wet mediums tend to sit on top quite happily. Try a wash of walnut ink with sea salt crystals sprinkled on the surface. Other wet mediums can also be used successfully but some, such as fluid acrylic paints, tend to leave the tissue a little stiff, although this does not seem to affect stitching into the piece.

As with the other tissue papers, foil can be bonded to the surface of heat distressable/polyester tissue using fusible webbing. Below, right you can see foil bonded to polyester tissue before scrumpling. The tissue was first coloured with disperse dyes.

The foil can also be used on the reverse of the transfer-dyed polyester tissue.

You also have the option of using a heat tool on the surface of this tissue paper, once it has been steamed, to create yet another unique effect, although the heat will make the piece shrink even further and the resulting fabric can be quite stiff.

∧ *Small bag created using heat distressable tissue coloured with disperse dyes.*

∨ *For this sample, the tissue was first coloured with disperse dyes and foil was then bonded to polyester tissue before scrumpling.*

> *Transfer-dyed polyester tissue becomes a rich metallic surface when foil is ironed onto the reverse.*

SECTION 3:
Magnificent Metallic Surfaces

Simple techniques with a polyester fabric can be so effective when the following method is used. The secret lies in the way that the colour migrates from the polyester to the metallic surfaces above it to produce unique metallic effects.

Foiled surfaces

This is a really exciting technique with many variations to create, depending on the choice of coloured background, the foil colour, the tissue paper and the embellishments on the surface.

The basic technique is very simple. You need a polyester fabric, dye colour, heat transfer foil, tissue paper and adhesive.

The foil is bonded to the dyed surface and tissue paper is glued on top. As the fabric starts to dry, it soaks the background colour through all layers to the surface in a very unpredictable way.

The resulting fabric can be stitched into by hand or machine. Beads or other embellishments can be stitched or glued to the surface.

If you intend to use the finished piece to create a book cover or similar and need to glue it to a background, make sure you cover any holes made by stitching with masking tape or the glue may seep through them to the surface.

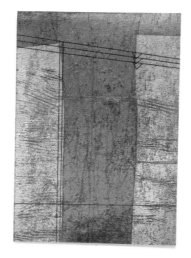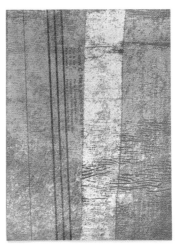

∧ *Foiling technique on pelmet Vilene background.*

Fabric

The background fabric needs to be polyester. Pelmet Vilene, Evolon and the heavier-weight Lutradur work really well, and you will get a reasonably good result on other polyester fabrics.

Having chosen your background fabric, you now need to colour it.

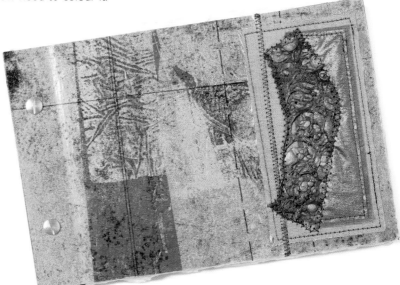

< *Foiling technique on Evolon background.*

Colouring agents

When choosing the colour for the background, keep the following points in mind:

- The colour of the foil being used: light-colour dyes will not show through a dark-coloured foil and a dark-colour dye may almost obliterate a light-coloured foil.
- For a 'rusty coloured' finish, use Mustard, Burnt Sienna or Rust Brown with a splash of Indigo Blue or Turquoise. This is perfect with a gold or copper foil.
- You will notice that, with the exception of pelmet Vilene, the colours on the polyester fabrics will dry very pale. Don't be tempted to add more dye as, once the tissue paper is applied and the fabric starts to dry, the migrating colours will be far more vibrant.
- Some dyes and colours will work better on one fabric than on another, so it's all a question of trial and error. Always test on a small piece first before going ahead with a larger project, and remember to keep notes and samples with your findings.

Procion dye powder

Mix a teaspoon or so of Procion dye powder with a pint of warm water. Fixatives are unnecessary as Procion dye will not fix to a polyester fabric. Adjust the quantities for a darker or lighter shade.

Brusho powders

These can be used full strength or watered down for a lighter shade.

Silk paints

Silk paints will work for this technique but you will need to use top-quality paints at full strength, which can make even a small project somewhat expensive.

It's a good idea to keep detailed notes on the colour and the product used and any alterations to the mix or the strength so that you can replicate that perfect piece you have created at a later date. Here's the method:

1. Lay the polyester fabric on a plastic-covered work surface and paint on the colouring agent. Use enough to cover the surface but don't saturate the fabric. It is the strength of the dye that is important and not the amount used. Leave the fabric to dry thoroughly on the plastic surface, which may take a day or two depending on the climate. This is especially important with polyester fabrics such as Lutradur and Evolon as a lot of the liquid colour will seep through the surface onto the plastic but will then be soaked back up again as the fabric is drying. Once the fabric has soaked up much of the dye, hanging it up will help it dry faster but it does need to be reasonably dry beforehand or the colour will all gather at the bottom end of the fabric. Using more than one colour can give a really exciting finished effect.

2. When the fabric is dry, iron fusible webbing onto the surface. A dense webbing, such as Bondaweb, is preferable for this technique as FuseFX, Gossamer Fuse and Misty Fuse are finer than Bondaweb. They do, however give a lovely lacy effect with the foil and this will allow more of the background colour to seep through. This gives a different effect that you might like, so try the technique both ways.

3. Iron the piece of foil onto the Bondaweb. Place the foil *shiny side up*, cover with baking parchment and iron for a few minutes on a wool–cotton setting. No need to press hard; it is the heat that releases the foil from the carrier paper, not the pressure. Leave to cool before removing the carrier paper.

The next stage is to bond the tissue paper to the surface with your chosen adhesive.

Tissue paper

It is recommended that you start with dressmaking pattern tissue paper because it's very easy to use and you are certain of a good result. Once you are familiar with the technique, you can move on to experimenting with other tissue papers.

You may wish to cut a piece of tissue from the dressmaking pattern that is totally unmarked but you will find that some of the markings usually disappear into the background and any that are left can actually enhance, or be used in such a way as to complement the design.

Iron out any heavy creases on the tissue and cut it slightly larger than the piece of coloured fabric.

> *For these delightful bodices, Evolon (light) was coloured with Procion dyes and foiled. Dressmaking tissue paper was then bonded to the surface before construction.*

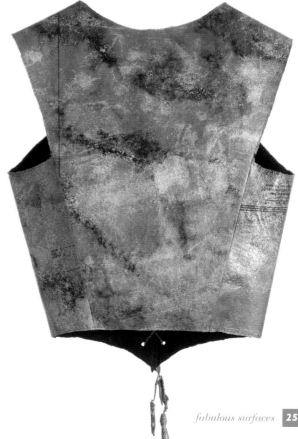

Adhesives

Polymer medium or fluid matt medium

These are products made by Golden and both work very well. The polymer medium leaves a gloss finish while the fluid medium leaves a matt finish. Both these products will give a finished top coat when dry. You will need to leave the finished piece of work to air-dry for a couple of days to get rid of any stickiness.

PVA glue

The PVA needs to be watered down, two parts PVA to one part water. It is too heavy to be used as it is and will drag on the surface and tear the tissue paper very easily. Adding water means the PVA will dry matt. If you prefer a shiny surface then give it another coat of full-strength PVA when the fabric is dry. This will stiffen the fabric slightly but should not cause too much of a problem.

Other adhesives that can be used include acrylic wax, gel or varnish, Mod Podge or decoupage glue.

You can see from the list of suitable adhesives that what you are aiming for is a white glue with the consistency of single cream and one that will dry clear.

∧ *This book cover was created using foiling techniques on pelmet Vilene. A further piece of the same fabric was overlaid with stainless steel mesh and used as an embellishment. Black embossing powder, thinly applied through a stencil, was heated, then lightly rubbed with Treasure Gold.*

Brush a very thin layer of your chosen adhesive onto the foiled surface. Do not use too much adhesive or the tissue paper will be very wet underneath and will tear far more readily. This is just to hold the tissue paper in position while you brush more adhesive on the surface. A wide brush, even on a small sample, is much easier to work with.

Lay the sheet of tissue paper on the top and use the brush to add more medium to the surface. Be reasonably generous with the adhesive.

Now use your fingertips lightly to really push the medium into the surface. Make sure the surface is always wet; if the medium starts to dry or gets tacky, the tissue paper will definitely tear.

If the tissue does tear then you have to make a very quick decision. Do you pull the whole piece off and start again? Or is the tear in such a place that you will be able to cover it with some form of embellishment or even make a feature of it? The other alternative is to cut a small piece of tissue to cover the tear but this will probably show up as a patch once dry.

There will be creases in the tissue paper, especially the finer ones; this is unavoidable. Use your fingers to work in the direction of the creases which will help to flatten them out.

∨ *This book cover was also created using foiling techniques. Here the edge was decorated with metallic brads.*

Keep applying more medium and gently rub it in well until the tissue paper has become transparent. The more you rub the glue into the fabric the more colour will come through to the surface.

It is very difficult to know when you have wetted the surface enough. Obviously, if the tissue starts to tear, then you know it is time to stop. Another indication is if you lift the fabric carefully and peep underneath you can see where the glue has already penetrated through to the back.

Now leave the fabric to dry for a day or two, preferably away from a heat source such as a radiator or the sun. If it dries too quickly, it will not work so well. You will then be able to see how the dye colour is brought to the surface through the fusible webbing, foil and tissue paper, giving a distressed look. It will now be clear why you do not saturate the fabric with the dye: too much colour and the foil and tissue paper will be totally obliterated.

Depending on the medium you have used, you may have to leave the fabric to air-dry for several days to get rid of any tackiness. Once the surface is totally dry, you can then embellish it however you wish. When you stitch, you will find that, regardless of the medium used for bonding, your machine needle will start to clog up with residue. Wipe the needle every so often with a damp cloth or a baby-wipe to prevent thread breakage or broken needles.

∧ Copper and turquoise foil were applied to this surface to give the impression of peeling paint.

< The sample on the left is made from pelmet Vilene coloured with Procion dye. On the right you can see the same piece after the tissue paper has been bonded to the foiled surface. The foil transforms the piece, giving it the appearance of metal.

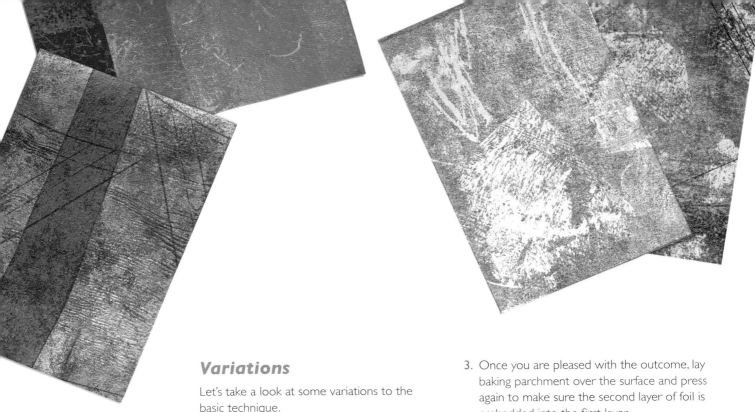

Variations

Let's take a look at some variations to the basic technique.

Foil strips

Place the foil in strips on the fused surface – this is a great way to use up all those odds and ends of foil! Overlap the edges of the foil to avoid any bare patches and cover with tissue as before.

Two-tone foil

Add depth with this method:

1. Fuse one layer of foil to the coloured surface, then add another layer of fusible webbing on top of the foil and press with the iron. You need to work quite quickly for this technique as the bonded surface needs to remain hot.

2. Peel the backing paper from the webbing as soon as it has melted and, with your foil still shiny side up, just dab at the surface here and there. Don't lay the foil down in the usual manner or the whole surface will be covered. Just keep dabbing and lifting – you are aiming for a patchy look.

3. Once you are pleased with the outcome, lay baking parchment over the surface and press again to make sure the second layer of foil is embedded into the first layer.

4. Now cover with tissue as before and you have a two-tone effect.

Choose your two colours of foil carefully to make sure they look good together. Using a shiny and a matt silver can look very effective, while a copper and turquoise colour scheme never fails to please.

Some more ideas for a two-colour effect:
- Using a different colour, draw a design on the foiled surface with a Hot Foil Pen, either before or after adding the tissue paper.
- Rub and crumple the second layer of foil, making sure there are lots of bare patches before applying it to the foiled surface; remember to add a second layer of fusible webbing beforehand. Alternatively, use a leftover piece of foil from another project.
- Machine stitch on the reverse side with Grilon thread – a heat dissolvable thread – in the bobbin. Apply the foil in the usual manner. As the iron melts the thread, the foil will only adhere to the stitched design. Alternatively just scatter snippets of the Grilon thread onto the previously foiled surface.

∧ *The top sample shows the foil ironed to the surface. The bottom sample is the finished piece with tissue paper bonded to the surface.*

1. Lay the cut-out shapes on top of the coloured polyester fabric. Cover with a layer of fusible webbing followed by foil before fixing the tissue paper to the surface with adhesive.

2. Take extra care with the tissue paper around the raised edges to prevent tearing.

3. Cutting the raised shapes from pre-coloured pelmet Vilene or Lutradur will allow the colour to come through to the surface.

4. Keep the foil from step one and bond this to coloured polyester with tissue paper on the surface.

The piece of polyester fabric the shapes have been cut from can also be utilised. Bond it to a background fabric, then add foil to the surface followed by tissue paper. You see – nothing is wasted!

Raising the surface with cut-outs

Using cut-out shapes underneath the foil adds further interest to the surface.

Pre-cut grungeboard shapes or shapes cut from pelmet Vilene, Lutradur or similar are perfect. Tools and cutting machines like the Sizzix, used by card-making artists, are also very useful as they are able to cut perfect shapes from pelmet Vilene or Lutradur. A soldering iron could also be used to cut out the required shapes.

∧ The top piece shows the raised cut-out shape, the bottom piece shows the use of leftover foil.

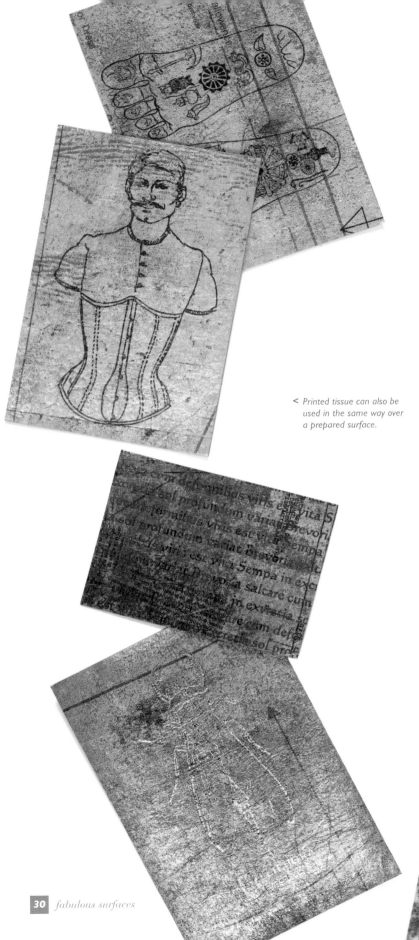

Printed tissue paper

The migrating colour trick can be used with the printed or drawn surfaces from page 14. Following the instructions, print on tissue paper with a laser printer, photocopier, inkjet printer or waterproof pen and adhere it to the foiled polyester surface with the adhesive of your choice.

The tissue paper can also be foiled before attaching it to the surface.

And once again, use the discarded piece of foil on top of a coloured polyester background before covering with tissue paper.

A foiled piece of tissue paper can also be added to a surface that has already been coloured and foiled with tissue paper added. As the surface will have previously been sealed, the colours from the background will not come through, so allowing the foiled text or design to stand really proud.

Experiment with other tissue papers

The tissue papers mentioned in the 'Materials' section give varying results. Not all of them work as well as dressmaking pattern tissue but exciting and different results are possible and they can be embellished further.

Layout paper, lightweight Lutradur and Vilene can also be used for this technique in place of tissue paper, with some really good results.

< *Printed tissue can also be used in the same way over a prepared surface.*

There are occasions when the results of this technique can be far from satisfactory. Maybe the glue had not been pushed into the surface adequately, maybe the piece dried far too quickly, or maybe you were just having 'one of those days'. In this case, further embellishments can certainly help but, if all else fails, try adding a wash of acrylic paint to the surface.

Without foil

This technique will also work quite satisfactorily without the foil, giving a totally different look. Just colour the polyester fabric in the same way and stick tissue paper to the surface with an adhesive. Further colour can then be added on top using any medium you prefer.

Sculpting

Another advantage of a polyester fabric is that the surface can be easily sculpted using a soldering iron to cut out motifs.

- Either draw the shape required onto the surface of the created fabric or work freehand.
- Work on a heat-resistant surface and take care at all times. Cut carefully around the shape.
- The tip of the soldering iron is very hot and the fabric may remain hot to the touch for several minutes after burning.
- Keep the negative cut-out as this can be used for another project.
- Treasure Gold, gilding cream or wax can be applied around the sculpted edges if desired for a neater finish.

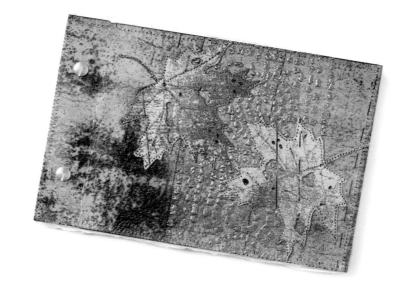

∧ *This background is dressmaking pattern paper bonded to acrylic felt then painted with fluid acrylic paints. Leaves were cut from tissue-covered pelmet Vilene and Evolon. Transformed into a book cover above.*

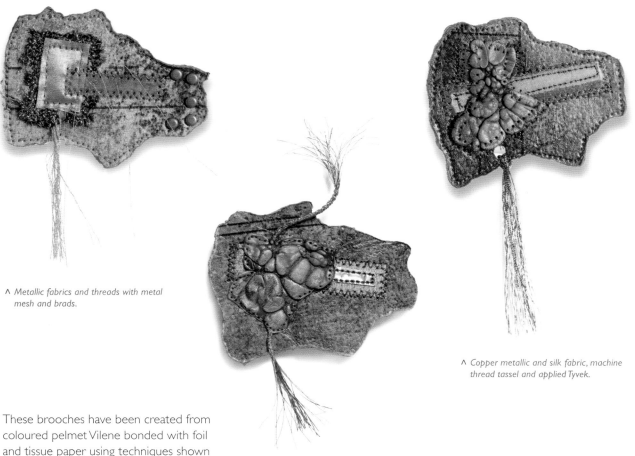

^ Metallic fabrics and threads with metal mesh and brads.

^ Copper metallic and silk fabric, machine thread tassel and applied Tyvek.

These brooches have been created from coloured pelmet Vilene bonded with foil and tissue paper using techniques shown in this section. The fabric created has then been backed onto a thick acrylic felt. The shape of the brooch was drawn on the surface before cutting out with a soldering iron.

^ Copper metallic fabric, turquoise metal shim, machine threads with coloured wire and applied Tyvek.

∧ Stainless steel mesh with metallic
threads and dangling chain.

∧ Copper metallic and silk fabric base.
Turquoise metal shim was decorated with
machine threads, mica flakes and beads.

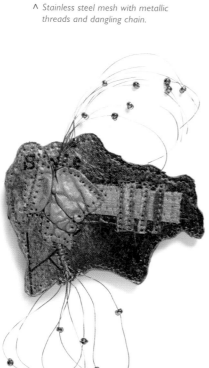

∧ Tyvek, copper shim and beaded wires.

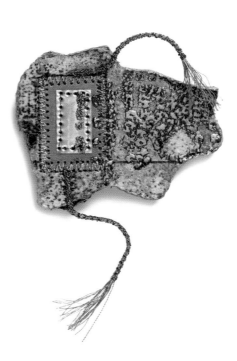

∧ Stainless steel mesh and shim, metallic
threads with wire. Heated embossing
powder was highlighted with Treasure Gold.

Metallic tissue paper

This product seems to be more of a cellophane than a tissue but the end results are just so exciting I really wanted to include it.

Metallic tissue on its own can be a bit bold. Why not try this technique to knock back the glare and make your sample look like a piece of aged metal?

The tissue will be bonded to a background and zapped so, before you start, consider the thread:

- A cotton thread on the surface will subsequently be covered with acrylic colour but the stitching will show, although this can be used to advantage.
- A metallic thread may also show through but can add to the effect.
- Polyester thread, as cotton, will be covered by the acrylic colour but can sometimes melt, leaving little blobs on the surface.

1. Use fusible webbing to bond a piece of metallic tissue to a background fabric. The background fabric needs to be a reasonably lightweight one that will burn back easily, so choose either Lutradur or Evolon. The fabric can be plain or coloured. The fusible webbing is not absolutely essential but it does make the metallic tissue easier to handle and prevents the tissue from melting back very quickly. Although you will still need to stitch the fabric before zapping, a base of Lutradur, lightly rolled with gesso, will also prevent too much meltdown. Crumpling the tissue before bonding to the background fabric also helps. Each method will give a slightly different look, so try them all until you have created the surface that appeals to you most.

2. Machine stitch in a loose grid pattern or a freehand circular motion. The stitching will also act as a resist to prevent the fabric from melting back too far once it is zapped.

3. Now place on heat protected surface and zap the reverse side with the heat tool. Melt back as much or as little as you wish. You will find that the fabric ends up at less than half the size it was before, and the shine on the foil has been knocked back considerably.

4. Once you have finished zapping the back, flip the piece over and lightly zap the front. This will make the piece lie flatter and will also dull down any shiny spots.

The surface is now ready to add colour.

Use fluid acrylic paints as they are transparent and will allow some of the metallic surface to shine through. The everyday acrylic paints tend to cover too thickly and you are not then able to appreciate the surface underneath.

> *Metallic tissue machine stitched to Lutradur, zapped and coloured with fluid acrylic paints.*

∨ *Metallic tissue bonded and then freehand machine stitched (bottom) to Lutradur before zapping.*

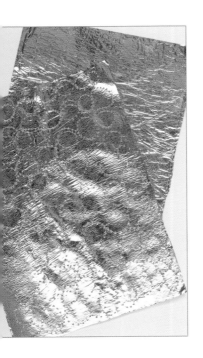

Tyvek, both the paper and fabric forms, can be used with the tissue for this technique and the resulting finish is very similar to the scrumpling technique on page 18. Work like this:

1. Stitch the metallic tissue directly to the Tyvek.

2. Place the stitched piece on baking parchment with the Tyvek side facing. Cover with another piece of baking parchment and press with a hot iron for a few seconds to melt the Tyvek. Zapping with a heat tool will give the same effect but is quite tricky to do as the Tyvek tends to curl up on itself.

3. Paint with acrylic paints either before or after stitching and melting.

> TOP: Metallic tissue, stitched to Tyvek paper, ironed to shrink and coloured with fluid acrylic paints.

BELOW RIGHT: Metallic foil stitched to Tyvek and zapped.

BOTTOM: Foil, coloured with acrylic paints, before and after zapping.

Paint the first layer and gently rub back the high spots with a baby-wipe or damp sponge to allow the metallic surface to shine through. Leave for a few minutes to dry, then add highlights in a second colour.

Transparent Red Iron Oxide with a dab of Paynes Grey makes an ideal rusty metal coloured surface.

After painting, give the surface another quick blast with a heat tool. This evens out the finish on the acrylic paints and renders the surface a dull matt colour, ideal for aged metal. It will also help to bond the paint to the foil surface.

The metallic tissue can be painted before zapping. It is easier to paint the tissue if it has already been bonded to the surface. Use a damp sponge or a dabbing motion with the brush to apply the paint. Do not over-brush or the paint will lift off. Leave to dry thoroughly if the piece has then to be stitched.

∧ The base of this hanging is a box canvas. Printed tissue paper was applied and coloured with fluid acrylic paints. A layer of rusted tissue paper was added and given a thin coat of Transparent Red Iron Oxide. The metallic tissue was stitched to Lutradur, zapped and coloured.

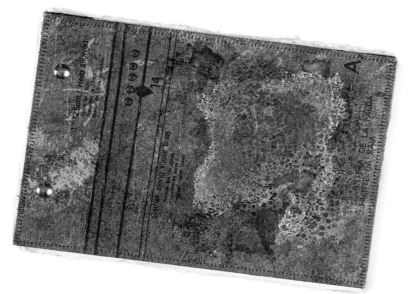

< Embossing powder, Treasure
Gold and white spirit were used
to create the effect on this
book cover.

∨ This sample shows the white
spirit technique worked on
metallic painted tissue paper
bonded to cotton muslin.

White spirit technique

This technique creates a unique metallic
surface using metallic paint on the tissue paper.
The interaction of the white spirit really creates
a fabulous look.

To create this surface you will need:
- tissue paper bonded to a
  background fabric
- metallic acrylic paints
- Treasure Gold
- white spirit
- Creative Sprays/
  Moonshadow Mists etc.

Here's the method:

1. Bond tissue paper to a background fabric
   using fusible webbing or another bonding
   agent. As the surface will be totally covered
   with metallic acrylic paint, an inexpensive gift
   wrap tissue is best suited for this technique.
   Choose your background fabric according
   to your finished project. Pelmet Vilene or
   heavyweight Lutradur would make a sturdy
   surface for a vessel, whereas muslin or thin
   cotton will make a soft flowing fabric ideal
   for wearable art.

2. Use metallic acrylic paint in your chosen
   colour to cover the tissue paper completely.

3. Allow the paint to dry thoroughly, then rub
   Treasure Gold quite thickly onto the surface.

4. Pour a small amount of white spirit onto a
   cottonwool pad and rub into the Treasure
   Gold, thus thinning the wax and spreading
   it all over the surface. Do not rub off the
   Treasure Gold completely, just smear it
   around the surface.

5. Before the white spirit evaporates, spray
   with a very generous amount of Creative
   Spray or similar; you do need to be really
   generous with the spray. Don't worry about
   any 'blobs' as they can give a really good
   effect. If necessary, once the spray dries, give
   it another coat. Using a different colour can
   work really well.

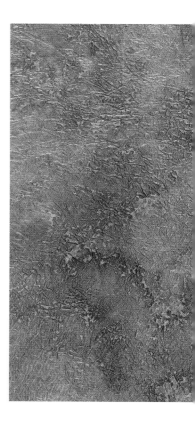

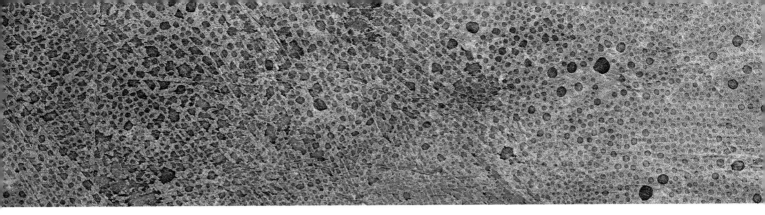

You may find that, once dry, the surface can feel powdery to the touch or may not be as glossy as you would like. In this case, use an acrylic spray varnish to lightly coat the surface. One thin coat should be sufficient or the resulting fabric may stiffen. Do not use a varnish or top coat that needs to be brushed on as the colours of the sprays will disperse and mix (although this too can give some very pleasing effects).

This technique will also work on tissue paper that has been coloured with fluid acrylic paints and sprayed with Creative Sprays as before. The surface will not need further sealing but, again, if a glossy finish is needed, spray with acrylic varnish.

< Pocket book and small bag made using the white spirit technique.

The method can also be used in conjunction with embossing powders to embellish a prepared surface. Here's how:

1. Brush a thin layer of glue on the surface and sprinkle ultra-thick embossing enamel (UTEE) on top.

2. Tip the excess back into the pot and heat the powder with a heat tool.

3. Have your rubber stamp or wooden block at the ready and, as soon as the UTEE starts to bubble, quickly press your stamp into it.

4. Leave to cool completely, then carefully remove the stamp. Rub a generous amount of Treasure Gold wax into the embossed surface before rubbing back with a cottonwool pad dampened with white spirit.

5. Spray liberally with Creative Sprays or similar and leave to dry.

A number of the techniques and samples in this book came about through trial and error while working on my original ideas.

I do hope they inspire you in the same way.

Enjoy!

∧ Samples of the white spirit technique worked on a foiled pelmet Vilene surface.

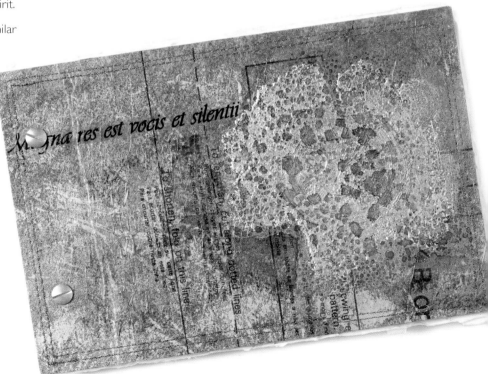

> This book was made by bonding tissue to a background fabric. It was then painted with metallic paint and waxed before it was distressed using white spirit.

∧ *Evolon light was coloured with Procion dyes before being bonded with gold coloured heat transfer foil. Dressmaking pattern tissue was then bonded to the surface. The more you iron this fabric, the more supple it becomes. Always iron between two sheets of baking parchment and never let the iron touch the surface of the fabric. The fabric was then cut to shape and stitched together before adding a lining of black acrylic felt. Rather than construct the bodice in the usual dressmaking fashion, the wrong sides were placed together and machine stitched before a soldering iron was used to cut around the whole shape and neaten the edges.*